Numerology

as taught by Yogi Bhajan

by

Dr. Guruchander Singh Khalsa, D.C.

Please direct all correspondence and inquiries to:

Radiant Light Press
1505 Llano Street
Santa Fe, New Mexico 87505
505-984-0934

Executive Editor
Production Manager
Gurujivan Kaur Khalsa

Editor and Proofreader
Siri Dharma Kaur Khalsa
Millis, MA

Typographer and Designer
Mary Kunard

ISBN: 0-9636752-0-6

Printed in the United States of America

Dedication and Thanks

It is with sincere appreciation and love that I dedicate this book to my spiritual teacher, Yogi Bhajan, Ph.D., and thank him for inspiring and guiding my in-depth study of numerology. He is the father of Humanology, from which this exploration of the human psyche comes. May God bless him for inspiring our awakening into this Age of Aquarius, and may his works forever prosper.

My love and thanks to Bibiji Inderjit Kaur, Ph.D., for her many personal sacrifices and her love for humanity. She and Yogi Bhajan continue to be the guiding lights in my life and in the lives of millions of Sikhs throughout the world. She will always be cherished for her kindness and wisdom.

Contents

Dedication and Thanks iii

Preface vii

Introduction 1

The Ten Bodies and the Eleventh Embodiment 7

The Five Positions of the Natal Numerology Chart 23

Interpreting the Numbers in the Positions 35

Yogi Bhajan's Natal Numerology Chart 59

Yogic Technologies for Mastering the Ten Bodies 61

Affirmations for the Aquarian Age 77

References 83

About the Author 85

Preface

I have had the pleasure of knowing Guruchander Singh for about 15 years, and the honor of working with him for the past two years. When we first started working on the new edition of this book, he told me that above all else, he wanted people to get this message from his books: God is Pure Love. The Universe is a Benevolent Process. Happiness is Our Birthright.

The ten bodies system of numerology presented in Guruchander's books is a liberating, empowering archetype that can help us realize this message and learn to manifest it in our lives. The yogic technology offers many powerful tools that can awaken us to our true nature and help us self-initiate into our own Godhood. We hope you enjoy this book and use it to spark your own insight and inner guidance.

Gurujivan Kaur Khalsa
May, 1993

I am Pure Love.

The Universe is a
Benevolent Process.

Happiness is
My Birthright.

Ang Sang Wahe Guru.

Introduction

Introduction

Ancient yogic science tells that human beings have ten bodies—soul body, negative mind, positive mind, neutral mind, physical body, the arc line, the aura, pranic body, subtle body, and radiant body. These bodies are our God-given, magnificent capacities as human beings. This system of numerology describes the ten bodies in detail and also gives a technology for learning to use them appropriately in any situation. We all have absolute access to all ten of our bodies; we just need to remember what we have always known.

Knowing how to access your ten bodies on command will serve you in very practical ways. Suppose that you're at a party and you begin feeling very insecure and afraid. A guilt-based response to these feelings would be: "God, I'm so insecure and scared. I'm such a mess. I'll never be successful if I act like this. I'd better go home before I make a fool of myself." This sort of self-talk ends up keeping you in a negative spiral and prevents you from moving forward. But with awareness of the ten bodies and their functions you could say to yourself: "There I go again, feeling insecure and afraid. My seventh and eighth bodies must be weak right now. I think I'll sit down for a while and do some deep breathing while I visualize myself having a big, strong aura. Then when I get home I'll do a yoga set that builds my aura."

The art and science of the ten bodies allows you to realize that any disharmony you experience can be identified and then restored to harmony. It's a practical model for understanding your own psyche, and it gives you a technology to practice that allows you to achieve bliss in your life. The real gift of the ten bodies system of numerology is how quick and simple it is—it teaches you to consciously access all the great, powerful parts of yourself so easily that you don't have to spend years (or lifetimes!) making mistakes or going through analysis or searching for just the right meditation to liberate yourself.

This book has 6 sections. First, there is a brief description of the ten bodies and the Eleventh Embodiment. Then there's a description of the five positions of the natal numerology chart, as determined from the individual's birth day. Your own natal numerology chart is a good place to start your study of numerology. Once you become familiar with this system, you can begin doing natal chart readings for your friends—it's a really fun way to better understand people at the same time that you inspire them. Section 4 is a detailed interpretation of each body in relationship to each of the five positions.

"Yogic Technologies for Mastering the Ten Bodies" is the key chapter of this book. It goes through each body and gives a number of techniques you can use to bring that body into consciousness and harmony. Why is this the key chapter? Because understanding is only the first step. You can analyze yourself and determine which of your ten bodies needs strengthening. But in order to really change your life, you have to do what it takes to master each body. That's where the technology comes in, and only you can do it for yourself.

I hope you enjoy this book and that you begin using ten bodies numerology to uplift yourself and others. This system is easy to understand, simple to use, and it gets quick results! It's a perfect tool for the Aquarian Age.

The Ten Bodies and the Eleventh Embodiment

The Ten Bodies and the Eleventh Embodiment

Your ten bodies—soul body, negative mind, positive mind, neutral mind, physical body, arc line, aura, pranic body, subtle body, and radiant body—are your God-given, powerful capacities as a human being. They allow you to be joyfully creative, obedient to your higher consciousness, and to see spirit in everyone. They let you evaluate the input of your mind to reach the compassionate, neutral place and they enable you to create sacredness, to sacrifice, and to live in balance. They make you intuitive and focused, secure and fearless, calm and subtle. They let you live life as a radiant, self-initiated, limitless being.

Each body has specific gifts that it gives you when it's strong, and certain deficits that surface when it's weak. The thing to remember is this: you can always strengthen any of your bodies. Once you become aware of a weakness in yourself, identify which body it corresponds to and then practice the technology that strengthens that body. It's very simple and direct. The Yogic Technology section has many suggestions of things you can do to strengthen each body.

In Sikh Dharma our ten Gurus correspond to the ten bodies. There are also key phrases and key words that go with to each of the bodies; learning these will help you tune into that space quickly and easily. In addition, the first seven bodies relate to the seven chakras.

First Body

SOUL BODY

Guru Nanak

First Chakra

"Creator"

creativity, humility, heart over head

Your soul body is the body that connects you to your inner God self, your inner infinity. It is the experience of the flow of spirit within yourself. When your soul body is strong, you lead with your heart instead of your head. When you master your soul body, you can come from a place inside yourself of great humility and creativity. You are so linked with your own infinity that you can relax into the flow of God energy and use it to create beauty in your life.

If your first body is weak, you may come from your head instead of your heart. You can end up feeling stuck and jammed up, not able to access your creative flow.

Second Body
NEGATIVE MIND
Guru Angad

Second Chakra
"Longing to Belong"
containment, obedience, connectedness

Your negative mind helps you give form to the creativity of your soul body by giving you the gifts of containment, form, and discernment. It also instills in you a longing to belong, which in its highest expression drives you to connect very deeply with your own God self. If your negative mind is underdeveloped, your longing to belong can cause you to get into inappropriate, self-destructive relationships because you are overly influenced by others; you aren't contained enough in your own center.

My soul number is a 2. Earlier in life, my problem was that I became so attached to people that it was pretty devastating. Two's start getting hurt when they're really young; they get so attached that they lose their own sense of self. For me the key was to really connect with my spiritual teacher, Yogi Bhajan, on a very deep level. When you connect with someone soul to soul you can't really be hurt because you're connecting from your own most secure and infinite place.

For years after I became a Sikh my 2 soul tormented me with a feeling that I wasn't connecting enough with Yogi Bhajan. Then one day I received a letter from him that said, "My dear son, you and I will always be one in our hearts." For someone with a 2 soul number, hearing this was complete bliss. That experience helped me understand what being a 2 means.

The second body gives you a lot of "negative" information about whatever comes up in your life so that you can provide for every contingency in order to protect yourself. Once I had formed a strong relationship with my own inner God self, I still had more work to do on my second body. I needed to learn to listen more to my negative mind so that I could use it as an asset. A strong second body serves you by giving you foresight and helping you to create contingency plans. It gives you the patience to be obedient to your own inner guidance.

If you have a 2 in your birth numbers you need to develop the habit of listening to and obeying your own inner voice; you need to practice feeling contained in your own Infinite Self.

Third Body
POSITIVE MIND
Guru Amar Das

Third Chakra (Navel Point)
"Devil or Divine"
positivity, equality, Thy will is my will

Your positive mind lets you see the positive essence of all situations and all beings. It gives you a strong will and allows you to use your power easily and humbly. It makes you naturally playful and optimistic, and gives you a good sense of humor. It makes your communication strong and direct.

If your positive mind is weak you may be overwhelmed by the input of your negative mind, which can be depressing and paralyzing. You may be angry and intolerant, or else hesitate to use your own power, your own heat, because you're afraid of the responsibility it brings or afraid that you might abuse it.

Fourth Body

NEUTRAL MIND

Guru Ram Das

Fourth Chakra (Heart Center)
"Cup of Prayer"
compassion, integration, service

Your neutral mind rules and integrates all parts of you. It evaluates the input of your negative and positive minds (and also of the rest of your bodies) and gives you guidance within nine seconds. It helps you access your soul and look with compassion on the whole play of life, which allows you to serve others from a place of great elevation. Your neutral mind can see the big picture and how all parts of your life have been necessary and perfect, because they have lead you to right where you are now.

If your neutral mind is weak you may have a hard time making decisions. You'll have the habit of feeling victimized by life because you don't know how to integrate you experiences and find meaning in them. You may have a hard time seeing beyond the polarities of life on earth and tuning into the great cosmic scheme of things.

Fifth Body
PHYSICAL BODY
Guru Arjan

Fifth Chakra
"Teacher, Balance"
balance, sacrifice, teaching

Your physical body is the body where the other nine bodies play out their parts. A strong fifth center gives you the capacity to sacrifice, to make sacred; it gives you the ability to balance all parts of your life. If your fifth body is strong you will be a flexible, eloquent speaker and you will naturally share what you know by teaching others.

If your fifth body is weak, your inner and outer realities will be out of balance—you won't know how to handle all the different aspects of your life in a flowing, balanced way. You may have trouble expressing yourself verbally, and you may be afraid to be in the position of being a teacher.

Sixth Body
ARC LINE
Guru Hargobind

Sixth Chakra (Third Eye)
"Person at Prayer"
protection, projection, justice

Your arc line is the balance point between the physical realm and the cosmic realm; it coordinates the inflow of cosmic knowledge from the upper chakras and integrates it through your first five bodies. By regulating the nervous system and glandular balance, your sixth body protects your heart center. You can use the intuition of your sixth center to protect yourself and its projective power to help you manifest whatever you want in your life. If your arc line is strong, you will be a natural meditator and have a very prayerful projection.

If your arc line is weak you may have glandular imbalances, which can lead to inconsistency in your moods and your behavior. You may be unfocused and unable to manifest your prayers. You also may not be using your intuition to protect yourself. (An in-depth discussion of the arc line can be found in the manual from Yogi Bhajan's fifth Men's Course—see page 83.)

Seventh Body
THE AURA
Guru Har Rai

Seventh Chakra (Tenth Gate)
"Platform of Elevation"
security, love, mercy

Your aura is the electromagnetic field around your body. When it's strong it acts as a container for your life force, and allows that life force to build up to a level where you feel completely confident and secure. Once you have this strong sense of security, you can truly open your heart and love yourself and others in an unconditional way. You are never threatened by someone else's energy because you always know who you are—you have realized that home is where the heart is and, therefore, that you are always at home. Your very presence will uplift other people. You may find that singing is a natural way for you to elevate yourself and others.

If your aura is weak you'll feel easily overwhelmed by whatever energy you are near. You may find yourself not being true to your own principles just in order to go along with everyone else. You may be defensive and over-reactive; you may try to find protection by isolating yourself from others.

Eighth Body
PRANIC BODY
Guru Har Krishan

"Finite to Infinity"
energy, fearlessness, self-initiation

Through your breath, your pranic body continuously brings life force and energy into your system. This allows you to feel absolutely fearless, fully alive, and totally at one with all creation. When your pranic body is strong and your breathing is deep and relaxed, nothing can bother you. You know how to use your energy when it's needed, and how to contain your energy when that's appropriate. You cherish every event in life and enjoy it to its fullest. By having a conscious relationship with an unconscious human function, the breath, you become self-initiated and self-illumined. Your very presence is healing to others because you carry so much pranic energy. In addition, a strong pranic body automatically balances the negative, positive, and neutral minds.

All disease starts with an imbalance in the pranic body. If your eighth body is weak, you may have constant low-level anxiety and chronic fatigue. You may try to get energy from food or stimulants. You may have a closed heart center because you just don't have enough energy to keep it open and flowing. You may be fearful and defensive.

Ninth Body
SUBTLE BODY
Guru Teg Bahadur

"Mastery or Mystery"
subtlety, calmness, mastery

Your subtle body helps you see beyond the immediate realities of life to the sublime universal play that lies beyond. When your subtle body is strong, you have great finesse and a powerful calmness. You always see beyond the obvious; nothing in life is a mystery to you. You learn quickly and master situations easily.

If your ninth body is weak you may be naive and easily fooled. You may be unintentionally crude or rough in your speech or behavior. You may be restless because you lack the peace that comes from having learned to flow with the way things are.

"One-Plus" Body
(Tenth Body)
RADIANT BODY
Guru Gobind Singh

"All or Nothing"

royal courage, nobility, radiance

Your radiant body provides you with a glorious, radiant sphere of light that extends for nine feet on all sides of your body. This sphere is brilliant and impenetrable—no outer negativity can penetrate it and all inner negativity is neutralized by it. A strong radiant body lets you project with royalty and grace. You exert a magnetic presence and command the respect of all who know you. You have great strength, determination, and stamina, and you always give 110%. Yogi Bhajan calls the tenth body "one-plus" because it's one—your soul body—plus your radiance.

If your tenth body is underdeveloped, you may be afraid of conflict. You may shy away from other people's attention because you are afraid of the energy and responsibility that come with the recognition of your inner nobility. You may feel ineffective and unable to come through in situations.

Eleventh Embodiment
COMMAND CENTER
Siri Guru Granth Sahib

"Eternal"

command center, completion, flexibility

Your eleventh embodiment is the command center from which you direct the play of the ten bodies. It allows you mastery of the physical realm and access to the entire spiritual realm. It endows you with complete flexibility of consciousness. From the command center, you are a completed, perfected being because you have mastered all ten bodies and you can use them in any combination at any time to excel in your life and to help uplift others. You can direct all parts of your being from an impersonal, expansive space that allows infinity to flow through you at all times.

For a more in-depth discussion of the ten bodies and the Eleventh Embodiment, and for stories about the Ten Sikh Gurus, please see the second book of this series, ***Tantric Numerology.***

The Five Positions of the Natal Numerology Chart

The Five Positions of the Natal Numerology Chart

Everyone is born with five numbers that represent the aspects of soul, karma, gift, destiny, and path. Understanding your own natal numerology is a really good way to start your study of numerology. Understanding someone else's natal numerology can make you more compassionate with that person.

Calculating the Five Positions of Your Natal Numerology Chart

The five positions of your natal numerology chart—soul, karma, gift, destiny, and path—can be easily calculated from your birth day by using the simple formula shown below.

When a number is more than one digit, such as 12 for the month of December, you add the two digits until you get one digit, e.g., 1 + 2 = 3. (Therefore the number for December is 3.) The number 10 doesn't reduce down to 1. Yogi Bhajan calls a ten "one-plus," so any

10 becomes 1+. The number 11 doesn't reduce down either; it stays as an 11.

Your **Karma Number** is the month number of the date you were born:

If you were born in _____	your karma number is:
January	1
February	2
March	3
April	4
May	5
June	6
July	7
August	8
September	9
October	1+ (10)
November	11
December	3
	(12 = 1 + 2 = 3)

Your **Soul Number** is the day number of the date you were born. (Remember, if it's a two-digit number other than 10 or 11, add the digits to reduce it down to one digit.) For example,

If you were born on _____	your soul number is:
January 1st	1
January 3rd	3
January 10th	1+
January 11th	11

January 12th	3
January 17th	8
January 19th	1+
January 20th	2
January 28th	1+
January 29th	11

and so on...

Your **Gift Number** is the sum of the last two digits of the year you were born. For example,

If you were born during _____ your gift number is:

19**45**	9 *(Add 4 + 5 to get 9.)*
19**52**	7 *(Add 5 + 2 to get 7.)*
19**58**	4 *(Add 5 + 8 to get 13, and then 1 + 3 to get 4.)*
19**64**	1+
19**74**	11

Your **Destiny Number** is the sum of adding together all the digits of the year you were born (the century number). For example,

If you were born in 1951:

Add 1 + 9 + 5 + 1 to get 16, and then reduce 16 down to a one-digit number by adding 1 + 6 to get 7. If you were born in 1951, your destiny number is 7.

If you were born in 1962:

Add 1 + 9 + 6 + 2 to get 18, and then reduce 18 down to a one-digit number by adding 1 + 8 to get 9. If you were born in 1962, your destiny number is 9.

If you were born in 1964:

Add 1 + 9 + 6 + 4 to get 20, and then reduce 20 down to a one-digit number by adding 2 + 0 to get 2. If you were born in 1964, your destiny number is 2.

If you were born in 1974:

Add 1 + 9 + 7 + 4 to get 21, and then reduce 21 down to a one-digit number by adding 2 + 1 to get 3. If you were born in 1974, your destiny number is 3.

Your **Path Number** is the final sum of adding together all the digits of your birth date. For example,

If you were born on 5/6/1961:

Add 5 + 6 + 1 + 9 + 6 + 1 to get 28. Then add 2 + 8 to get 10. If you were born on May 6th, 1961, your path number is 1+.

If you were born on 11/14/1977:

Add 1 + 1 + 1 + 4 + 1 + 9 + 7 + 7 to get 31. Then

reduce the 31 down to a one-digit number, 4. If you were born on November 14, 1977, your path number is 4.

If you were born on 8/2/1972:

Add 8 + 2 + 1 + 9 + 7 + 2 to get 29. Then reduce the 29 down to 11. If you were born on August 2nd, 1972, your path number is 11.

Yogi Bhajan writes a person's natal numerology chart in the following formula:

$$\frac{\text{Day of Birth}}{\text{Month of Birth}} = \frac{\text{Last 2 digits of Birth Year}}{\text{Century Number}} \quad \text{Path}$$

If your birthday is 9/17/52, the formula is:

			(gift)		
(soul)	8	=	7	7	(path)
(karma)	9		8		
			(destiny)		

The Meaning of the Five Positions

After you determine your birth numbers, you will have five numbers that indicate your primary strengths and weaknesses. This is a good place to begin working on your ten bodies. Whatever bodies are represented in your birth chart, begin strengthening them and becoming more conscious of them. In the case of the soul, karma, and path numbers, start developing those bodies more. In the case of the gift and destiny numbers, be sure that you're actually using those God-given strengths as much as you can.

> For convenience, we will refer to the numbers of the birth chart by their position. For instance: If you have a 9 in the karma position, 9 is your karma; if you have a 3 in your gift position, 3 is your gift; if you have an 11 in the path position, 11 is your path, and so on.

The Soul Position

Your soul number is your link to your soul, the part of you that connects you to the cozy, loving God within you, which gives you deep peace and harmony. It is the creative, flowing part of you; you experience your soul when you let your heart rule instead of your head. Once you know how to consciously connect with your soul, you no longer experience abandonment, you no longer feel separation from God. You are able to operate from a place of true inner security.

Your soul number usually indicates a weak link; you need to learn to consciously access and master it so it can serve you. For instance, if you have a 7 soul number, you need to develop your auric body in order for that body to help you connect with your soul. When you come into conscious relationship with the body represented by your soul number, that body will always serve you under stress by connecting you to your soul.

The Karma Position

Karma is external disharmony, conflict experienced in the world. Your karma number indicates one of your weak spots—you will probably find yourself experiencing the negative, disharmonious aspects of that body. For instance, if you have a 2 in the karma position, you may have such an intense longing to belong that you ignore danger signals and end up in self-destructive relationships. Once you have mastered the body represented by your karma number, you will find that all your external relationships are harmonized; you will automatically recognize someone's frequency and adjust to it in order to have a graceful interaction.

It may also be part of your karma to have the opportunity to meet your spiritual teacher. Karma starts you on your spiritual path, your Dharma. Yogi Bhajan says, "Where there's Dharma, there's no karma." Once you have engaged in a spiritual discipline, that discipline begins to harmonize your internal state and your external world so that you no longer have external disharmony, karma.

After you have practiced your Dharma for a while, you come to the transition stage, *Shakti Pad*, where you experience a struggle between your inner voice and your entrenched karmic patterns. This usually also manifests as distrust of your spiritual teacher, who is the external reflection of your inner voice. You'll know you've made it through Shakti Pad when you have accepted the guidance of your own inner voice as a way of life. Then you'll begin experiencing your life as a flow of divinity, which is the stage of *Sahej Pad*.

The Gift Position

Your gift number is God's gift to you in this lifetime. The body indicated in the gift position is a natural talent and asset for you. It gives you strength; you can rely on it; it will support you when you are under stress. For instance, someone with a 5 gift can do a lot of physical exercise to relieve stress.

When I do someone's natal numerology I often ask, "Do you accept gifts easily?" Some people don't use the strengths and assets of their gift body. If you aren't doing any spiritual discipline, you may be so unconscious of your own energy that you don't know how to access your gift. Once you engage your consciousness, your gift will begin to flow and you will become very creative with using it. For instance, if you have an 8 gift you may be fearful and feel weak, but once you begin to strengthen your pranic body, you'll realize what a reservoir of courage and energy you have available to you.

The Destiny Position

The body represented by your destiny number shows what capacities you have worked on and developed in many other lifetimes, what well-developed talents you have brought with you into this life. You may be manifesting either the positive or negative qualities of that body, depending on how conscious you are. The destiny number is usually one of the strongest aspects that people see in you. It is also referred to as "Master of Many Lifetimes."

The Path Position

You can go sit in a cave and become a great yogi, but in order to complete the circle of life, you also need to fulfill your mission here on earth. Your path number indicates what you have to do in this lifetime in order to feel spiritually fulfilled, in order to feel divine. When you master the body indicated by your path number, you'll feel that you're finally doing what you're supposed to be doing. Your path number shows you your channel for serving others and for teaching others how to fulfill themselves.

There are several stages in spiritual evolution. During the stage of *Sahej Pad*, you give up the struggle with your inner guidance and begin to experience the flow of your divinity. You begin living from your soul and trusting your very deepest self. Once you are permanently identified with your soul voice and absolutely locked into that way of being, you have reached the stage of *Sat Pad*. This is when you really begin to live you path number. Your path number is the most natural way for you to share with others how to find fulfillment. When you master your path number, you begin to experience feedback from the universe that you are fulfilling your mission here on earth.

Interpreting the Numbers in the Positions

Interpreting the Numbers in the Positions

Each number in your natal numerology chart describes a body and its capacities, and indicates whether you are using that body as an asset or experiencing its more negative side. As you begin to tune into the ten bodies and the five positions more, you'll probably come up with your own creative interpretations of the numbers in the positions.

Basically, the karma, soul, and path numbers are usually experienced as challenges. Until you have come into a conscious relationship with that body, you may find yourself primarily exhibiting its negative characteristics. The gift and destiny numbers usually manifest in a more positive way, and as you begin to further develop those bodies, they become even stronger assets.

Often people will have the same number in more than one position. For instance, if you have an 8 karma number and an 8 gift number, it could mean that you need to accept and develop your natural talent for having energy and being fearless, or else you will experience a lot of fear and mistrust in your external environment and relationships.

Interpreting the Numbers

If you have a 9 destiny number and a 9 path number, it could mean that you need to rededicate yourself to the subtlety and mastery you have developed in many lifetimes so that you can serve others with those talents. Having the same number in the gift or destiny position as you have in one of the more challenging positions may mean that you are lazy about using your natural talents, and that your life is pushing you to consciously access them. Again, as you become more familiar with the bodies and the positions, you can use your own intuition and insight to interpret these sorts of combinations.

> **Karma** needs to be neutralized by Dharma, by engaging in a practice that harmonizes your internal world and your external world.
>
> **Soul** needs to be accessed by becoming cozy with your own inner guidance.
>
> **Gift** needs to be accepted and strengthened through engaging in a conscious practice. Remember that in order to fully access your gift number, you have to be willing to receive a gift.
>
> **Destiny** is what you have developed throughout many lifetimes and how other people see you. You need to develop a strong, conscious relationship with that body in order to manifest your destiny fully.
>
> **Path** is how you use all your fulfilled potential in order to serve others on the path to consciousness.

REMEMBER: You can live in the positive side of any body. Your natal numerology chart is only a starting place; any challenges that are indicated in it are places to begin developing more consciousness. Turn any deficit into a wonderful asset; you have within yourself the capability to fully manifest all the gifts of all ten bodies and to use them with flexibility and joy.

THE NUMBER 1

Soul Body

"Creator"

creativity, humility, heart over head

Karma of 1:

If your karma number is 1, your bottom line is always creativity; you need to have your creative energy accessible to you and working for you in order for your external world to be in harmony. Once you are in a conscious relationship with your soul body, you will automatically manifest the humility that comes from being in that state. Until you have strengthened your relationship with your soul body, you may tend to relate to other people from your head. In order to be happy in your external relationships, you need to start coming from your heart rather than from your head. Any technology that harmonizes the soul body will help you come into harmony with all your external dealings.

Soul of 1:

If you have a 1 in the soul position, when you're under stress you may get into circular arguments with yourself because you're coming too much from your head. You may be too attached to using logic to solve problems, which ends up being a frustrating dead end. Once you come into a more conscious relationship with your soul body, you will be so internally creative that you'll know how to use all your tools—including logic—in a balanced, integrated way to solve any problem. Any practice that strengthens the soul body will help you balance your head and heart so they can work peacefully together.

Gift of 1:

If you have a 1 in the gift position and you are accepting and accessing your gift, you are creative and humble; you know how to balance head and heart. You have a strong flow of creative energy and know how to bring ideas into reality. Anything that strengthens your soul body will help you use your gift more fully.

Destiny of 1:

If you have a destiny number of 1, you have been very creative and humble in other lives; you have developed a very strong relationship with your soul body, and other people see you as coming from your heart in a balanced way. Any technology that strengthens the soul body will help you manifest your destiny even more fully.

Path of 1:

If you have a path number of 1, you need to be very creative in order to feel deeply fulfilled in this lifetime. You express your deepest self through creativity and you use that creativity to help others find their fulfillment. If you aren't relating to your consciousness and living in harmony with your own soul, you will be dominated by your head and unable to access your heart. Any practice that develops the soul body will help you to begin living your path number.

See page 65 for technologies that strengthen the Soul Body.

THE NUMBER 2

Negative Mind

"Longing to Belong"

containment, obedience, connectedness

Karma of 2:

If your karma number is 2, you may be very vulnerable in your relationships because your have such a great longing to belong. You may try to find fulfillment through connecting on a sexual level, which will only lead to pain until you learn to connect on a soul level. You may also get taken advantage of in business relationships, because you are doing business in order to make a connection or gain a friend. You need to start forming relationships with people who are conscious and aware so that you can learn to pattern your relationships that way. Any technology that strengthens your relationship to your negative mind will help you become more self-contained.

Soul of 2:

If your soul number is 2, you can find peace only by connecting to your own inner God self. You need to practice feeling this connection and should pay special attention to your relationship with your spiritual teacher or guide. Your best protection is dwelling in your own self-containment. Any technique that strengthens your negative mind will serve you well.

Gift of 2:
If your gift number is 2, you have a natural understanding of boundaries and are able to approach each person in a way that is graceful and acceptable. You also have the ability to see the potential dangers in any situation, and to use that information to protect yourself and others. Any practice that strengthens the negative mind will increase your ability to use your gift fully.

Destiny of 2:
If you have a destiny number of 2, you have developed common sense and self-containment through many lifetimes. People see you as being level-headed and practical. They find you easy to talk to and to connect with; you are a good friend. Any discipline that strengthens the negative mind will help you live your destiny number strongly.

Path of 2:
If you have a path number of 2, you will find fulfillment by dedicating yourself to a life of obedience to your own inner voice and connection with your soul. You need to exhibit these qualities clearly in order to help liberate others from their human loneliness. Any technology that strengthens the negative mind will help you fulfill your life purpose.

See pages 65—66 for technologies that strengthen the Negative Mind.

THE NUMBER 3

Positive Mind

"Devil or Divine"

positivity, equality, Thy will is my will

Karma of 3:

If you have a 3 in the karma position, you need to strengthen your positive mind; your negative mind may dominate you with an over-awareness of the negativity in your relationships and your environments to the point that you're paralyzed. You need to cultivate your ability to see the light and the goodness around you. Any technique that strengthens your positive mind and your navel point will empower you to be balanced and happy.

Soul of 3:

If your soul number is 3, you may have the tendency to talk to yourself negatively. When you are processing something mentally or emotionally, you may find yourself focusing on all your own negative aspects and getting into the rut of negating yourself. You may also distrust your own power because you are afraid of its negative consequences. Any practice that strengthens the positive mind and the navel point will help you see that your own light is the same as the Infinite Light and that your own power is a gift from the Infinite.

Gift of 3:

If you have a gift of 3, you can always find something positive in any person or any situation; you are cheerful and hopeful and have a good sense of humor. You are able to overlook people's flaws and encourage their better qualities. You are comfortable using your own power because you know that you won't abuse it. Any technology that strengthens the positive mind and the navel point will help you more fully use your gift.

Destiny of 3:
If you have a 3 in the destiny position, you are seen by other people as being a very positive asset in any situation. You are seen as exerting your power in a balanced, conscious way. Any technique that develops the positive mind and the navel point will help you live your destiny number fully.

Path of 3:
If you have a 3 path number, you find your life's fulfillment by dedicating yourself to being equally concerned for all beings. Any practice that strengthens the positive mind and the navel point helps you to live in the flow of seeing the light in all and serving the consciousness of all.

See pages 66—67 for technologies that strengthen the Positive Mind.

THE NUMBER 4

Neutral Mind

"Cup of Prayer"

compassion, integration, service

Karma of 4:

If you have a 4 in the karma position, you may have a hard time being neutral; you may be extremely opinionated and enjoy arguing about what's right and what's wrong. Any technology that strengthens the neutral mind will help you accept life as you find it without the need to judge it.

Soul of 4:

If you have a 4 soul, you may be very indecisive; you may torment yourself trying to come to conclusions while you mind jumps back and forth between what seem to be two polarities. Any practice that strengthens the neutral mind will help you develop the ability to analyze any input and get quick, accurate, wise answers.

Gift of 4:

If you have a 4 in the gift position, you are a naturally wise person; you have a talent for seeing the play of life in a neutral, humble way. You serve others with compassion and know how to find meaning and worth in any situation. Any technique that strengthens the neutral mind will help you live your gift more fully.

Destiny of 4:

If you have a 4 destiny number, people are drawn to you for wise counsel. You are known for your neutrality and insight into life. You see the play of life so clearly and have such compassion for it that you never judge harshly. Any practice that develops the neutral mind will help you live your destiny fully.

Path of 4:

If you have a path number of 4, you need to serve with love and pure selflessness in order to realize your fulfillment. You need to help other people find meaning and worth in their experiences, so that they too are liberated from duality. Any technique that strengthens the neutral mind will help you live your life's path.

See pages 67—68 for technologies that strengthen the Neutral Mind.

THE NUMBER 5

Physical Body

"Teacher, Balance"

balance, sacrifice, teaching

Karma of 5:

If 5 is your karma number, you may not have fully accepted the sacredness of your physical body. You may be ignoring its needs and not taking care of it. Perhaps you indulge yourself by eating too much food and not getting enough exercise, or you drive your body too hard by not resting enough. You may find it hard to sacrifice; people might see you as too self-interested, especially in business situations. Any practice that strengthens your physical body and helps you settle lovingly into it will harmonize your external circumstances and relationships.

Soul of 5:
If you soul number is 5, you may have a hard time keeping an internal balance, which can reflect in imbalance in all areas of your life. You might have a hard time giving adequate time and energy to all different parts of your life—personal time, business time, family time, social time, exercise, rest, eating and not eating, etc. You may also be reluctant to share what you know with other people. Any technology that strengthens your physical body will help you come into an internal and external balance so that all parts of your life have their appropriate place.

Gift of 5:
If your gift is 5, you have a comfortable relationship with your physical body; you know how to care for it and keep it strong so it can support you. All parts of your life exist in an easy balance with each other; you are able to sacrifice immediate gratification in order to facilitate greater future harmony. You enjoy sharing what you have learned with others, and have a natural gift for teaching and for powerful speech. Any technique that strengthens your physical body will help you use your gift more fully.

Destiny of 5:
If you have a destiny number of 5, people see you as being well-balanced and capable of sacrificing present gain for future harmony. People look to you as a teacher; what you have to say has a powerful influence. Any practice that strengthens the physical body will help

you access these talents that you have developed through many lifetimes.

Path of 5:
If your path number is 5, you will find fulfillment in this lifetime by teaching others with your example, by personifying balance and sacredness so that others can model from you. Any technology that strengthens the physical body will help you live your path and fulfill your life's mission.

See pages 68—70 for technologies that strengthen the Physical Body.

THE NUMBER 6

The Arc Line

"Person at Prayer"

protection, projection, justice

Karma of 6:
If 6 is your karma number, your power to project may be weak; you may find it hard to be consistent; you may not be able to live up to your word. You may have a hard time focusing, and therefore be unsuccessful in drawing what you want into your life. Any technology that strengthens your arc line and third eye will improve your projection and your one-pointedness so that your external world begins to reflect your deepest prayers.

Soul of 6:

If your soul number is 6, when you are under stress you may not be able to hold your own center, which can make you feel confused and overwhelmed. Any practice that strengthens your arc line and third eye will help you hold your focus and contain yourself in your own being.

Gift of 6:

If 6 is your gift, you have strong powers of concentration and are able to project your deepest prayers, drawing all good things into your life. Your intuition is strong and you use it to protect yourself and others. Any technique that strengthens the arc line and third eye will help you use your gift fully.

Destiny of 6:

If your destiny number is 6, you have developed your powers of concentration and projection through many lifetimes; you are a natural meditator and you emanate a sense of prayerfulness. People see you as being very one-pointed and effective. Any practice that strengthens the arc line and third eye will help you access these talents.

Path of 6:

If your path number is 6, the best expression of your divinity is for you to be powerfully prayerful and meditative. You can serve the consciousness of others by being in that concentrated part of your being. Any technology that develops the arc line and third eye will help you live your life's fulfillment.

See pages 70—71 for technologies that strengthen the Arc Line.

THE NUMBER 7

The Aura

"Platform of Elevation"

security, love, mercy

Karma of 7:

If 7 is your karma number, you may find yourself feeling overwhelmed by your external environment and your relationships. You may be easily confused in situations where there is a lot of stimulation around you, because your aura is letting too much in and not containing you enough. Any practice that strengthens the aura will help you feel your own integrity and security so that nothing outside you can sway you.

Soul of 7:

If your soul number is 7, you may have a hard time uplifting yourself internally; it may be hard for you to get your spirit moving and to feel that life is good and exciting. Any technology that strengthens the aura will allow you to reach the state where you can elevate yourself with ease.

Gift of 7:

If 7 is your gift, you have a natural talent for being uplifting; your own strong sense of security allows you to truly love and be merciful with yourself and others. You naturally bring light and love into any situation. Any technique that strengthens the aura will help you use your gift fully.

Destiny of 7:
If 7 is your destiny number, you have developed your own inner security throughout many lifetimes and have a great capacity for love and mercy. People are automatically elevated by your presence. Any practice that strengthens the aura will help you access these natural talents.

Path of 7:
If 7 is your path, in order to be fulfilled in this life you need to develop your capacity for unconditional love and absolute mercy. In order for you to dwell in your own divinity, you must dedicate yourself to elevating others and giving them inspiration. Any technology that strengthens the aura will help you live your path.

See page 70 for technologies that strengthen the Aura.

THE NUMBER 8

Pranic Body

"Finite to Infinity"

energy, fearlessness, self-initiation

Karma of 8:
If your karma number is 8, you may feel as if you never have enough energy to deal with all the demands in your life. Your inability to access your prana may keep you from having an infinite vision of what you need to do in your life, what steps you need to take to get from where you are to where you want to be. Any technique that

strengthens the pranic body will allow you to become a "master planner," you will have the energy to prevail in any situation.

Soul of 8:

If your soul number is 8, fear may be dominating your internal processes. You may find yourself making excuses for your life that are based on fear. This fear drains your energy and keeps you from being happy and fulfilled. Any practice that strengthens the pranic body will give you boundless energy and make you fearless. Then you will be able to feel the expansiveness of infinity.

Gift of 8:

If 8 is your gift, you are fearless and have great reserves of energy. Nothing can get in your way, because you never experience lack of anything. You are a natural strategist and long-term planner, and an asset in any endeavor. Your very presence brings life and energy to others and gives them hope. Any technology that strengthens the pranic body will help you fully use your gift.

Destiny of 8:

If your destiny is 8, you have developed fearlessness through many lifetimes; nothing stops you; you can carry anything through to the end. People see you as being very energetic and find your presence to be healing and enlivening. Any practice that strengthens the pranic body will help you access these natural qualities.

Path of 8:

If your path is 8, you will find fulfillment in life by bringing joy, energy, hope, and healing to others. You will be living your divinity when you help other people find their own inner fearlessness, their own inner vitality. Any technique that strengthens the pranic body will help you to live your path.

See pages 71—73 for technologies that strengthen the Pranic Body.

THE NUMBER 9

Subtle Body

"Mastery or Mystery"

subtlety, calmness, mastery

Karma of 9:

If 9 is your karma number, you may not be tuning into how to create grace and harmony in your external relationships and environments. You may be ignoring the subtle cues around you, which can make you naive and gullible. You may not be willing to do what it takes to master certain tasks and skills that are important to you. Any practice that develops the subtle body will put your environments and relationships into the flow of grace and beauty. Doing that practice for 1,000 days in a row will instill within you the experience of mastery.

Soul of 9:

If your soul number is 9, you may be very hard on yourself. You may find yourself miserable because so much of life seems mysterious to you; you're not accessing your own inner understanding. Any practice that strengthens the subtle body will allow you to begin treating yourself with grace and gentleness. You will start giving yourself the time and space to recognize your own inner mastery.

Gift of 9:
If 9 is your gift, you are very accurate and precise; you are able to access deep understanding of everything; you know the unknown. You have such grace and calm that you are like a lotus flower on the water, riding along and enjoying the waves. Any technology that strengthens the subtle body will help you use your gift fully.

Destiny of 9:
If your destiny number is 9, people see you as being very masterful in any situation. You have developed the capacity through many lifetimes to learn systems and understand patterns quickly. You are able to let people know things in a graceful, subtle way. Any practice that strengthens the subtle body will help you access your mastery of the known and unknown.

Path of 9:
If your path is 9, you will find your life's fulfillment by helping other people open up to the subtleties of the flow of life. Your divinity will be best expressed when you exhibit your mastery of the known and unknown with grace and calmness, in a way that soothes people. Any technology that strengthens the subtle body, especially if you practice it for 1,000 days, will help you to walk your path.

See page 73 for technologies that strengthen the Subtle Body.

THE NUMBER 1+
(10)

Radiant Body

"All or Nothing"

royal courage, nobility, radiance

Karma of 1+:
If your karma number is 1+, you may be wishy-washy in your external relationships because you're afraid of conflict. You may deliberately down play your own radiance because you're not comfortable standing out and being noticed. You may lack stamina and determination. Any practice that strengthens the radiant body will help you claim your strength and radiance so that you can create an environment that supports your inner nobility. Then you will be able to give 110% to all your endeavors.

Soul of 1+:
If 1+ is your soul number, under stress you may talk to yourself in a disempowering way. You may convince yourself that you just can't make things happen, that you are ineffective, that you won't follow through. A 1+ soul number can make you manifest the "nothing" part of "All or Nothing." Any practice that strengthens the radiant body will allow you to give your all to life, to live it with courage and brilliance.

Gift of 1+:
If 1+ is your gift you have a natural radiance and nobility that carries you through any situation. You have such strength and determination that you can see any project through to the end, and you will

always be the person who puts 110% into it. Nothing can bother you because your radiant body neutralizes any internal or external negativity. Any technique that strengthens the radiant body will help you live your gift more fully.

Destiny of 1+:

If 1+ is your destiny number, people see you as a majestic, noble being of light. Your automatically exert a magnetic presence that draws people's attention to you. You have developed royal courage and determination throughout many lifetimes, and these attributes elicit the respect of those around you. Any practice that strengthens the radiant body will help you manifest your destiny.

Path of 1+:

If your path number is 1+, you will find your fulfillment through using your innate majesty, courage, and determination to uplift and encourage others. Your divinity will be best expressed by allowing others to use your powerful, radiant presence as a source of inspiration. Any technique that strengthens the radiant body will help you live to your highest aspirations for your life.

See page 74 for technologies that strengthen the Radiant Body.

THE NUMBER 11

The Command Center

"Eternal"

command center, completion, flexibility

Karma of 11:

If your karma number is 11, you may not be relating to your mastery of the physical realm. You may always be worried about practical problems—money, physical appearance, possessions. Any technology that strengthens the command center will allow you to claim your mastery of the physical realm.

Soul of 11:

If your soul number is 11, you may have internal conflict about mastering your life; you may find yourself confused about how to take command of your own being. Any practice that strengthens the command center will allow you to let your highest consciousness rule your life so that you can manifest your divinity.

Gift of 11:

If 11 is your gift, you have the natural flexibility and mastery to express any of your ten bodies in the optimum way at any time. You know how to ride the waves of the play of life and access any part of yourself appropriately. Any technology that strengthens the command center will strengthen your ability to exhibit mastery in all realms.

Destiny of 11:

If 11 is your destiny, your destiny has been written and will never change. People find your presence to be a constant reminder of Infinity; your consciousness of your own God self never wavers. Any technology that strengthens the command center will help you live this destiny.

Path of 11:

If your path number is 11, you will find your life's fulfillment by becoming a constant reminder and example of infinite, creative, flexible consciousness. Your divinity will be best expressed when you use your gifts and power to draw people into their own highest consciousness, when you use your presence to inspire and elevate. Any practice that strengthens the command center will allow you to live your path.

See page 75 for technologies that strengthen the Command Center.

For a more in-depth description of the ten bodies and the Eleventh Embodiment, please see the second book of this series, ***Tantric Numerology****.*

Yogi Bhajan's Natal Numerology Chart

Yogi Bhajan's birthday is August 26, 1929.

Using his formula,

Day of Birth	=	Last 2 digits of Birth Year	Path
Month of Birth		Century Number	

we can see that his natal numerology chart is:

8	=	11	10
8		3	

Yogi Bhajan has two eights in his numbers, both his soul and his karma. In order to avoid manifesting the negative side of these numbers, he would have to master his pranic body. He is definitely the Master of the pranic body; his energy level seems limitless; he works about 20 hours a day or more. His consciousness is so linked to Infinity that he is absolutely fearless.

Yogi Bhajan's Chart

His gift number is 11, which means that he is naturally endowed with the mastery of all his bodies; he can direct their play and manifest their perfection in all situations. He has taught us to connect with the Siri Guru Granth Sahib, which is the vibrational representation of that perfection.

Yogi Bhajan's destiny number is 3. For many lifetimes, he has been the provider for all. He sees all who come to him in their infinite goodness and relates to all beings equally and with positivity. Guru Amar Das was the third Sikh Guru; he was very devoted to caring for people. I always think of 3 as the "Big Papa" number.

And finally, Yogi Bhajan's path number is 1+. He fully expresses his divinity and serves his mission here on earth through his radiance and his nobility. Even when he's dressed in running shoes and shorts, he has a magnificent, kingly presence. Yogi Bhajan has guided the Khalsa throughout the world to develop and thrive and to claim our radiance.

Yogic Technologies for Mastering the Ten Bodies

Yogic Technologies for Mastering the Ten Bodies

About ten years ago I first began to tune into my own numerology. I saw that I had a karma number of 9, which means that I have to achieve mastery in order for my life to be harmonious, but I didn't yet know what that really meant. Then one day I went to a class where Yogi Bhajan was talking about how to make changes in your life. He said, "Forty days of a meditation begins to break the old habit. Ninety days puts a new habit into your subconscious."

I was beginning to wonder what mastery meant when he continued, "One hundred and twenty days locks a new habit into the subconscious so that it is an automatic pattern from that point forward." Then Yogi Bhajan looked right at me and said, "After 1,000 days you will be a master." Well, that's all I needed to hear. I knew right then that I was going to do a meditation for 1,000 days; I just didn't know which one. Then one day I was looking through a yoga manual and I saw a meditation called Chandra Mudra, and I knew that it was the meditation I would do for 1,000 days. It was an incredible meditation—it really opened me up.

Yogic Technologies

What do you have to do in order to master something? You have to do it over and over and over again, until you go through the highs and the lows and the boredom of it, until you get into the very essence of it. You go through layers and depths of understanding, and after 1,000 days you know all the subtlety.

Below are some very beautiful technologies to help you strengthen your ten bodies and the Eleventh Embodiment. Doing any of them for any amount of time is a good start—it's kind of like a kaleidoscope: if you move even one piece of the pattern, the whole pattern shifts. If you can do a specific technology for 40, 90, 120, or 1,000 days, that's even more powerful. Your intention, your prayer, your projection, and this technology together constitute a very powerful formula for transformation.

Some of the resources listed below are yoga manuals and some are Sikh religious books. The yoga manuals are listed on page 83. The Sikh religious books—the *Nitnem*, the *Amrit Kirtan*, and the *Siri Guru Granth Sahib*—are available for reference at any Sikh Gurdwara. Many of the Sikh prayers have been translated into modern American English and can be found in the book *Peace Lagoon*—see page 83.

Mastering Your Soul Body

- Take psyllium seed husks and chlorophyll to keep your first chakra functioning smoothly.
- Do the Exercise Set for Balancing Head and Heart in *Kundalini Yoga for Youth & Joy*.
- Do the three meditations for the heart center in the *Kundalini Meditation Manual for Intermediate Students*.
- Recite Jap Ji Sahib every day for 1,000 days. (This Sikh prayer can be found in *Peace Lagoon* or a Sikh *Nitnem*.)
- Study the life and teachings of Guru Nanak.
- Sing any *shabad* written by Guru Nanak or about Guru Nanak. (The *shabads* (sacred songs) of the Gurus can be found in the *Siri Guru Granth Sahib* , the *Amrit Kirtan*, and the *Peace Lagoon*—see page 83.)

Mastering Your Negative Mind

- Drink cucumber juice to balance your bladder and kidneys.
- Chinese herbs and acupuncture are very effective in healing the second body.
- Do the following meditation:

  Sit in a comfortable position with your hands relaxed on your knees and your fingers in Gyan Mudra (touching the tips of your index fingers to the tips of your thumbs). Close your eyes and concentrate on the point between your eyebrows. Inhale, and as you exhale chant, "Wahe Guru,

Wahe Guru, Wahe Guru, Wahe Ji-o" out loud, eight times each breath. Repeat this for 31 minutes. Inhale, hold your breath for a moment, then exhale and relax.

- Do the Exercise Set for the Lungs and the Blood Stream in *Kundalini Yoga for Youth & Joy.*
- Recite Shabad Hazaare every day. This prayer can be found in the *Nitnem* or in *Peace Lagoon.*
- Meditate on and read about Guru Angad; also sing Guru Angad's shabads or songs about him.
- Study the life and teachings of Guru Angad.

Mastering Your Positive Mind

- Compose affirmations about the things in your life you want to change. Make a subliminal tape of yourself saying the affirmations over and over. Listen to the tape on an auto-reverse tape player while you sleep. Remember, when you make an affirmation, say in a very positive, loving way what you *do* want in your life. Don't say what you *don't* want. (For a more complete discussion of the power of affirmations, see the second book of this series, *Tantric Numerology.*
- Do the meditation Eliminating Thoughts You Dislike in the *Kundalini Meditation Manual for Intermediate Students.*
- Do Nabhi Kriya, which can be found in *Kundalini Meditation Manual for Intermediate Students.*

- Do the Exercise Set for the Lungs and the Blood Stream in *Kundalini Yoga for Youth & Joy*.
- Do Stretch Pose:

  Lie on your back on a firm, cushioned surface. Stretch your legs forward with feet together and toes pointed, and extend your arms parallel along your hips (but not touching them) with your fingertips pointing towards your toes. Raise your feet and head six inches off the floor and focus your eyes on your toes. Hold this position for one to three minutes (or longer), using long, deep breathing or breath of fire (see description below). When you're finished, relax for a few minutes. Then bring your knees to your chest and hold them with your arms while you gently rock back and forth on your spine.
- Read Anand Sahib daily. This prayer can be found in the *Nitnem* or in *Peace Lagoon*.
- Play any shabad by Guru Amar Das. Meditate on or sing "Ardaas Bhaee, Amar Das Guru, Amar Das Guru, Ardaas Bhaee. Ram Das Guru, Ram Das Guru, Ram Das Guru, Sachee Sahee."
- Study the life and teachings of Guru Amar Das.

Mastering Your Neutral Mind

- Wear white clothes and eat white food.
- Do the meditations Kirtan Kriya or Shabad Kriya in *Kundalini Meditation Manual for Intermediate Students*.

- Do cross-crawl exercises:

  Lie on your back on a firm, cushioned surface. Inhale and raise both your left leg (bent at the knee) and your right arm (held straight) up to 90 degrees. As you exhale, lower them and raise the right leg and the left arm (in the same positions) up to 90 degrees. Use a moderate speed, not too slow and not too fast. You can start by doing cross-crawls for one minute and work up to as long as you want.
- Do the Exercise Set for the Lungs and the Blood Stream in *Kundalini Yoga for Youth & Joy*.
- Read from the *Siri Guru Granth Sahib*.
- Sing regularly any shabads written by Guru Ram Das or the five shabads about Guru Ram Das, which can be found in the *Amrit Kirtan*.
- Study the life and teachings of Guru Ram Das.

Mastering Your Physical Body

- Do aerobic exercise for at least a half hour three times a week (an hour is even better).
- Touch the thumb of your right hand to the small finger of your right hand and then make the same mudra with your left hand (Buddhi mudra). Chant the mantra "Ra ra ra ra; Ma, ma, ma, ma; Rama, rama, rama, rama; Sa ta na ma."
- Do Breath of Fire:

  Sit comfortably with a straight spine. Rest your hands on your knees, palms up, with your fingers in gyan mudra (touching the tips of the index fingers to the tips of the thumbs). Breathe fairly rapidly (about 2 or 3 breaths per second) through your nose, while you pump your navel point and abdomen—pulling them sharply inward on the exhale, and pushing them out during the inhale. Your chest should be relaxed. When you're finished, inhale deeply and hold the breath while you pull the energy up into your higher centers. Then exhale and relax.

This is a balanced breath with no emphasis on either the inhale or the exhale. Try thinking of it as one continuous breath being pulled in and out. You won't hyperventilate if you don't breathe through your mouth. Start practicing breath of fire for no more than three minutes at a time, and work up to 31 minutes or more.

- Do the following meditation:

  Sit in a comfortable position, close your eyes nine-tenths of the way and focus on the point between your brows or at the tip of your nose. Put your hands at your heart center in prayer pose and chant "Ad Guray Nameh" as your hands go out to a 60 degree angle; then chant "Jugad Guray Nameh" as you bring your hands back to the heart center; then chant "Sat Guray Nameh" as your hands go back up to a 60 degree angle in front of you, and then "Siri Guru Devay Nameh" as your hands go back to the heart center. Continue for 31 minutes. At the end of that time, inhale deeply, hold your breath and feel the energy. Exhale and relax.

- Do the exercise set Transforming the Lower Triangle to the Higher Triangle in *Kundalini Meditation Manual for Intermediate Students*.

- Read Sukhmani Sahib every day. This prayer can be found in the *Nitnem* or in *Peace Lagoon*.
- Sing any shabad about Guru Arjan or any shabad that Guru Arjan wrote.
- Study the life and teachings of Guru Arjan.

Mastering Your Arc Line

- Do the exercise set Ajnaa Stimulation Kriya in *Keeping Up With Kundalini Yoga*.
- Do the meditations on pages 45 and 57 of the *Men's Manual: Part V*.
- Do Sodarshan Chakra Kriya:

  Sit in a comfortable position with a straight spine. Rest your hands on your knees, palms up, with your fingers in gyan mudra (touching the tips of the index fingers to the tips of the thumbs). You can either close your eyes all the way and focus at the brow point or else close them nine-tenths of the way and gaze at the tip of your nose. Block your right nostril with your right thumb and inhale deeply through your left nostril. Hold your breath in and mentally vibrate "Wahe Guru," making it into three beats: "Wha Hey Guru." Vibrate it 16 times, for a total of 48 beats, on each inhale. With each beat, gently pump your navel point, for a total of 48 pumps. Then block your left nostril with your right index finger and exhale through your right nostril. Repeat the cycle. At the end of the kriya, inhale and hold your breath. Stretch your hands up, stretch your spine, and shake your hands and upper body vigorously. Exhale and relax.

Start doing this kriya for 11 minutes a day and build up gradually to 31 minutes, 62 minutes, or two-and-a-half hours daily. You may have difficulty holding your breath for the full 48 beats at first. You can start with eight "Wahe Guru('s)", which is 24 beats and 24 pumps of the navel, and build up as your lung capacity and stamina increase.

- Study the life and teachings of Guru Hargobind.

Mastering Your Aura

- Eat sweet, yellow foods and wear citrine and amber.
- Do any meditation where you focus on your tenth gate (the crown of your head).
- Do the exercise set Balancing the Aura in *Kundalini Yoga for Youth & Joy*.
- Do the Meditation for the Divine Shield in *Kundalini Meditation Manual for Intermediate Students*.
- Do the exercise set on page 59 of the *Kundalini Yoga Sadhana Guidelines* manual.
- Read and study the life and teachings of Guru Har Rai.

Mastering Your Pranic Body

- Do anything that encourages diaphragmatic breathing, such as aerobic exercise and singing.

- Do any meditation for healing.
- Do the exercise set on page 18 of *Kundalini Yoga for Youth & Joy*.
- Do the meditation on page 71 in the *Men's Manual: Part IV*, and the meditation Wahe Guru, Wahe Guru, Wahe Guru, Wahe Ji-o. (See "Mastering Your Negative Mind" above.)
- Do Sodarshan Chakra Kriya. (See "Mastering Your Arc Line" above.)
- Do Breath of Fire. (See "Mastering Your Physical Body" above.)
- Do Camel Pose:

  Sit on your heels and hold your ankles. Come up on your knees, arching your hips up and forward. Let your head gently drop backwards. Do long, deep breathing or breath of fire (see above for description). Hold this position for three minutes, then inhale, hold your breath a few seconds, and exhale. Slowly come back down to sitting on your heels. If your back muscles feel tense, balance them by sitting with your feet stretched out in front of you and bending slowly forward to hold your toes for a few minutes.
- Do Baby Pose:

  Sit on your heels and bend forward slowly until your forehead is resting on the ground in front of your knees. Let your arms lie on the floor along-side your lower legs, palms up and relaxed. Close your eyes and focus on your third eye. Settle into the position and do deep, easy breathing. You can start with three to five minutes, and work up to more.

- Do Nauli Kriya: (Do this kriya with an empty stomach.) Stand with your feet shoulder-width apart and your knees slightly bent. Bend at the waist slightly (keeping your lower back straight) and rest your hands above your knees with the thumbs on the inner thighs. Inhale deeply through your nose. Then exhale with moderate force, press your hands into your legs, and pull your stomach up and in. Keeping your breath out, pump your stomach and diaphragm in, up, and out six times. Inhale, exhale, and repeat. Start by doing this for one minute, and work up to more.
- Study the life and teachings of Guru Har Krishan.

Mastering Your Subtle Body

- Wear nice clothes and jewelry and tune into the subtlety and grace of it.
- Do any meditation, yoga set or other discipline for 1,000 days.
- Do Wha Guru Kriya in *Kundalini Meditation Manual for Intermediate Students.*
- Do "Breath Meditation Series for Glandular Balance" in *Kundalini Yoga Sadhana Guidelines.*
- Sing shabads about Guru Teg Bahadur.
- Study the life and teachings of Guru Teg Bahadur.

Mastering Your Radiant Body

- Do Guru Gobind Shakti Mantra Meditation in *Kundalini Yoga Sadhana Guidelines*.
- Do Archer Pose for 11 minutes on each side:
  Stand with your right leg forward and with the knee bent forward over your toes. Extend your left leg straight back with the foot flat on the ground at a 45-degree angle to the front foot. Raise your right arm straight in front at shoulder level, parallel to the ground, and make a fist as if grasping a bow. Pull your left arm back as if pulling a bowstring back towards your shoulder. This will create a tension across your chest. Fix your eyes on the horizon above your right fist. Breathe long and deeply. Hold this position for three to five minutes. Then inhale deeply, exhale, switch sides, and repeat.
- Do Varuyas Kriya in the *Kundalini Yoga Sadhana Guidelines*.
- Chant "Godinday, Mukanday, Udaaray, Apaaray, Hariang, Kariang, Nirnaamay, Akaamay."
- Recite Jaap Sahib every day. This prayer can be found in the *Nitnem* or in *Peace Lagoon*.
- Sing any shabad about or by Guru Gobind Singh.
- Study the life and teachings of Guru Gobind Singh.

Mastering Your Command Center

The technology of many Sikh devotional practices in the Gurdwara is actually based on yogic science. When you bow before the Siri Guru Granth Sahib, your arc line touches the arc line of the Siri Guru Granth Sahib; immediately its regenerative, vibratory effect starts expanding, clearing, and balancing your ten bodies. Any time you spend in the Gurdwara—whether meditating or chanting or doing *seva* (devotional service) or reading from the Siri Guru Granth Sahib—recharges you and expands you into all your infinite capacities.

- Read from the *Siri Guru Granth Sahib* every day.
- Meditate or chant before the Siri Guru Granth Sahib.
- Perform seva in the Gurdwara.
- Chant the Mul Mantra:
  Ik ong kaar, Sat Naam, Kartaa Purakh, Nirbhao, Nirvair, Akaal Moorat, Ajoonee, Saibhang, Gur Prasad, Jap: Aad Sach, Jugaad Such, Hai Bhee Sach, Naanak Hosee Bhee Sach.

Affirmations for the Aquarian Age

Affirmations for the Aquarian Age

It is your birthright to be the perfected, ultimate human being. You have complete access to all ten bodies and you are joyfully and creatively flexible in using them. In every situation you use the skills of your ten bodies to uplift yourself, your environments, and the people around you. You are always learning and growing, flexing and flowing with the dance of the Universe. You are able to communicate and reach the depth of any human being. You have absolute humility—you see how small you are in the infinite universe and you also know that you *are* the infinite universe.

The yogis and sages talk about *Naam*—the power of the word. Now is the time for us to consciously employ Naam, to re-create the way we talk to ourselves about who we are and what life is about. "I love myself. I am love. I am a totally secure, fearless, masterful, and subtle being. I can use any of these qualities at any time in my life. I am so creative and flexible that I can help others to see their demeaning beliefs and pull themselves out of it."

In the Sikh lifestyle, doing the *banis,* the daily prayers, creates a daily practice of talking to yourself in an infinite way. Using consciously devised, loving affirmations is another very powerful way to re-create your self-talk. Below are affirmations for each of the ten bodies and the command center. You can use them, or use your own insight and creativity to custom design your own affirmations.

> I am joyfully creative and humbly cozy with my own soul.
>
> I always feel connected to the guidance of my higher self and I relate to all boundaries with grace and respect.
>
> I see the spirit in every person and the benevolence of the Universe in every situation. I allow the power of Infinity to flow through me and guide my actions.
>
> My compassionate heart allows me to find meaning and worth in all my experiences and to clearly see the play of life. I serve with an attitude of gratitude.
>
> All parts of my being and my life are balanced and in harmony. I deeply know the sacredness of all experience and I share that awareness with others.
>
> I allow myself to integrate the cosmic realms into my body and into my life. I know everything that has ever been known and I am

guided and protected by my intuition. The one-pointedness of my prayer draws all good things to me.

I dwell cozily within my true self and feel the security and safety of my own identity. I am loving and merciful with myself and all other beings.

I am fully conscious of my breath. I have endless reservoirs of energy and lifeforce and I am deeply relaxed and trusting. I initiate myself into my own ecstasy.

I know and trust the flow of life and I gracefully play my part. I dwell in the depths of reality with great patience and calmness. I am the master of my own Universe.

I am a golden radiant being who lives in majesty and nobility, with fearlessness and finesse. I fully exhibit my soulful self externally.

I have total conscious access of all my powerful talents and capabilities, and I use them creatively and joyfully. I live my life in the consciousness that I am an infinite being in my identity and in all my endeavors and achievements.

References

Khalsa, Dr. Guruchander Singh, D.C. 1992, 1993. *Tantric Numerology*. Santa Fe, New Mexico: Radiant Light Press.

Harbhajan Singh Khalsa Yogiji. 1979. *Man to Man, Part IV: Growing as a Man*. Eugene, Oregon: Khalsa International Trading.

Kundalini Research Institute. 1981. *Man to Man, Part V: The Real Strength of the Man*, ed. Siri Dharma Kaur Khalsa. Eugene, Oregon: Khalsa International Trading.

Kundalini Research Institute. 1974. *Sadhana Guidelines for Kundalini Yoga Daily Practice*, ed. M.S.S. Gurucharan Singh Khalsa.

Kundalini Research Institute. 1975, 1977, 1978, 1984. *Kundalini Meditation Manual for Intermediate Students,* ed. M.S.S. Gurucharan Singh Khalsa.

Kundalini Research Institute. 1978. *Slim and Trim Yoga Exercises for Women*, ed. Sat Kirpal Kaur Khalsa, Ph.D.

Kundalini Research Institute. 1980. *Keeping Up with Kundalini Yoga,* ed. M.S.S. Gurucharan Singh Khalsa and S.S. Gurubanda Singh Khalsa.

Peace Lagoon, compiled by Sardarni Premka Kaur. 1971, 1973, 1974. Los Angeles, California: G.T. International.

Yogi Bhajan. 1983. *Kundalini Yoga for Youth and Joy,* ed. S.S. Dr. Sat Kirpal Kaur Khalsa. Eugene, Oregon: 3HO Transcripts.

***Tantric Numerology* is available from Radiant Light Press. All other publications listed above are available from Khalsa International Trading. Please write or call:**

K.I.T. Catalog
2545-D Prarie Rd.
Eugene, OR 97402
1-800-359-2940

About the Author

Dr. Guruchander Singh Khalsa was born and raised in Texas. He received his B.A. in business administration from Southern Methodist University in 1972, and his Doctor of Chiropractic degree from Pasadena College of Chiropractic in Pasadena, California, in 1982.

Guruchander Singh began studying yoga with Yogi Bhajan in 1972 and joined the American Sikh community a year later. In addition to his training in chiropractic, he has studied other forms of oriental healing for the past 20 years. He is Director of GRD Health Clinic in Santa Fe, New Mexico, which offers chiropractic, acupuncture, massage therapy, and other natural healing arts.

Guruchander Singh is a minister of Sikh Dharma International, and has responsibility for the Central Domain of Sikh Dharma in the United States. He served as Chairman of Khalsa Council, the Congress of Sikh Dharma International, from 1991–93.

Dr. Khalsa is also the author of *Tantric Numerology*, the second book of his healing trilogy. He is currently at work on the third book of the series. He and his wife and daughter live in the Sikh community in Espanola, New Mexico.

For copies of Guruchander's books, for information about seminars, or to be put on our mailing list, please write or call:

Radiant Light Press
1505 Llano Street
Santa Fe, New Mexico 87505
505-984-0934